The Romantic Movement
and the Study of History

by

H. R. TREVOR-ROPER

*Regius Professor of Modern History
in the University of Oxford*

The John Coffin Memorial Lecture
delivered before the University of London
on 17 February 1969

UNIVERSITY OF LONDON
THE ATHLONE PRESS
1969

Published by
THE ATHLONE PRESS
UNIVERSITY OF LONDON
at 2 *Gower Street, London* WC1

Distributed by Tiptree Book Services Ltd
Tiptree, Essex

Australia and New Zealand
Melbourne University Press

Canada
Oxford University Press
Toronto

U.S.A.
Oxford University Press Inc.
New York

D14
T73

485 16206 7

Printed in Great Britain by
WILLIAM CLOWES AND SONS LTD
LONDON AND BECCLES

The interests of John Coffin, in whose memory this lecture was founded, were evidently various. They included literature, philosophy, history. Today it is the turn of history. But it seemed to me, when I sought for a title, that, in order to commemorate him, I should not be too austerely historical: that I should examine before you some aspect of history which partakes also of literature and philosophy; and for this reason, I have chosen as my subject, or at least for my title—for it is a great mistake to give away too much in a title—the Romantic Movement and the Study of History.

Every age has its historical philosophy, and such a philosophy is seldom, if ever, the work of historians only. Historians follow each other along professional grooves, refining their predecessors' techniques; but they do not create new philosophies. These are brought in from outside, either by the immediate impact of events or from more general intellectual revolutions. The new science of Machiavelli underlay the 'civil history' of the seventeenth century. The new sociology of Montesquieu made possible the 'philosophic history' of the eighteenth century. I am concerned today with the external intellectual force which made the next great historical change: which changed the philosophy of the eighteenth-century historians—Hume, Robertson, and Gibbon—into the philosophies of their nineteenth-century successors—Macaulay, Michelet, Ranke.

I say, 'the external intellectual force', for of course there were external non-intellectual forces too. Most obvious of all was the impact of events. In the last years of the eighteenth century Enlightened Europe was convulsed, first by the French Revolution, then by the French conquest. In those convulsions the ideas of the past century were damaged beyond repair. When the goddess Reason was set up as the idol of a sanguinary dictatorship and French 'Enlightenment' was carried over the continent by military force, the charms of both quickly faded. In England, in Germany, in Spain, old native traditions, even superstitions, acquired a new force, a new respectability. Man did not live, it was discovered, by reason alone. The old, customary organs of society, the old established beliefs, which had seemed so contemptible to the rationalists of the Encyclopaedia, now acquired a new dignity. The greatest of English whigs, Edmund Burke, became the European prophet of a new conservatism: the conservatism of a society which must protect its living organs against the frivolous surgery of fashionable or interested theorists. In his last years, the greatest of eighteenth-century historians, who had never accepted the radicalism of the Encyclopaedia—for like Burke himself, he was a disciple of Montesquieu—would hail Burke's *Reflexions on the French Revolution* as 'an admirable medicine against the French disease. I admire his eloquence, I approve his politics, I adore his chivalry, and I can even forgive his superstition.'[1] And the greatest of nineteenth-century historians would declare that the historical studies of his time had developed 'in opposition to the tyranny of Napoleonic ideas'.[2]

But if the immediate convulsions of Europe caused men to appreciate anew the previously insulted traditions of their own society, another movement, independent in its origins, invested those traditions with a positive, romantic glow. Already, in the middle of the century, that movement had begun. It began, or or least one great stream of it began, in Scotland. In 1760 James Macpherson, a man of questionable morals both in literature and in politics, published his *Fragments of Ancient Poetry Collected in the Highlands*, the precursor of his more famous fabrication, the *Fingal* of 'Ossian'. In 1765, in England, Thomas Percy established a less brilliant but more lasting fame with his

---

[1] *The Letters of Edward Gibbon*, ed. J. E. Norton (Oxford, 1956), iii, 216.
[2] Leopold v. Ranke, *Zur Eigenen Lebensgeschichte* (*Sämmtliche Werke*, Leipzig, 1890, vols. 53–54), p. 47.

Reliques of Ancient English Poetry. With these two works, a new fashion was launched: a romantic cult of primitive society, primitive literature; and it was this cult which, transformed by political events unimagined in the 1760s, would help to create a new historical philosophy.

At first, the reaction of historians to this new literary or philological fashion had been cool. To a disciple of Voltaire, the Dark and Middle Ages were dark indeed. They were the ages of gothic barbarism and superstition and nothing that came out of them could have any virtue at all. Even to a disciple of Montesquieu, such literature, however interesting for the light that it shed on the society which produced it, was of no intrinsic value; and anyway, was it authentic? 'Something of a doubtful mist still hangs over these Highland traditions', wrote Gibbon, 'nor can it be entirely dispelled by the most ingenious researches of modern criticism. But if we could, with safety, indulge the pleasing supposition that Fingal lived and that Ossian sung, the striking contrast of the situation and manners of the contending nations might amuse a philosophic mind.'[1] 'I see', Hume wrote to him on reading these words, 'you entertain a great doubt with regard to the authenticity of the Poems of Ossian. You are certainly right in so doing. . . .'[2] In his private conversation, Hume was more outspoken. He would not believe in the authenticity of Ossian, he said, though fifty bare-arsed Highlanders should swear to it.

So spoke the voice of reason in 'the full light and freedom of the 18th century'. But as the full light faded and the ordered freedom dwindled, the artificial glow and the anarchical liberty of the past appeared more attractive. Ossian, that thin, tawdry figment of the Highland *débâcle*, might excite the smile of Gibbon, the ridicule of Hume, the rage of Johnson, but abroad his fortune was fabulous. He would become the inspiration of

[1] Gibbon, *Decline and Fall of the Roman Empire*, ch. vi (ed. Bury, 2, 129).
[2] *Letters of David Hume*, ed. J. Y. Greig (Oxford, 1932), ii, 310.

Herder,[1] the idol of Germany. Napoleon himself would carry the book as his *bibelot* on his campaigns: it was to him, he would say, as Homer had been to Alexander, Vergil to Augustus; and at Malmaison his empress would decorate her elegant new palace with Ossianic *bric-à-brac*, busts of the mythical Highland poet, paintings of his ghost welcoming in Elysium the heroes of her husband's wars. Meanwhile, in a more modest way, Bishop Percy too was enjoying his posthumous triumph. His *Reliques of Ancient English Poetry*, having also inspired Herder in Germany, fell into the hands of a Scotsman more influential even than Macpherson: Walter Scott.

Macpherson and Scott, the Highlander and the Lowlander of Scotland, these are the makers, direct or indirect, of the new romanticism which would change the character of historical study. At first it may seem parochial to say this; for after all, romanticism had many sources: why then should we deduce it from this private northern spring? But in fact, this is not, I think, too gross a simplification. Scotland, in the eighteenth century, was one of the intellectual capitals of Europe. The direction of its energies might change, but the power behind them was the same. The same social chemistry which released, in one generation, the genius of Hume and Adam Smith, formed, in the next, as its secondary product, the genius of Scott. Nor was Scott in any way parochial. Rooted though he was in the Scottish Border, whose every valley and stream, castle and peel-tower he knew so well, he was a cosmopolitan, a European too. We should not forget that long before he became known in Europe, years before he decided to abandon the law for literature, Scott had studied not only Ossian (whom he had the taste to despise) and Percy (whom he revered), but the romantic literature of Europe; that he learned Italian to read, every year, Ariosto and Boiardo; that he pored over

---

[1] J. G. Herder's essay, *Über Ossian und die Lieder alter Völker*, was published in *Deutsche Art und Kunst*, 1773.

Bartholin and studied Old Norse in order to read the Scandinavian sagas[1]; and that, as a young lawyer in Edinburgh, he learned German in order to enjoy the poets of *Sturm und Drang*: that his earliest published works were translations of Bürger's poems and Goethe's *Goetz von Berlichingen*.

But for all his cosmopolitan range, Scott was also intimately wedded to his own country. He was a Scotsman, and a Borderer. Indeed, this local loyalty lay at the base of his cosmopolitanism. The Scottish Enlightenment, like every era of enlightenment, had its social foundations. Its great writers—Hume, Robertson, Ferguson, Adam Smith—directed their minds to the progress of society not merely because they had read Montesquieu, but because their own society provided them (as English society did not provide Englishmen) with a case-history for the application of Montesquieu's social laws. They saw before them, simultaneously, the old static, introverted society of pre-Union Scotland and the new transforming energies released by the renewed post-Union contact with the world. The dynamics of progress were visible before them,[2] and they delighted in that progress. A generation later Scott looked more nostalgically at the same process. For him, the old society, whose relics had seemed barbarous to his predecessors, had acquired, in retrospect, a new charm. Just as Macpherson had idealised the vanishing tribal society of the Celts and turned Hume's 'bare-arsed Highlanders', 'the bravest but the most worthless' of men, into romantic heroes, so Scott was captivated by the archaic Border society of which, by now, only the memory survived. For centuries the Borders, on the Scottish side, had been a closed, static, almost fossil society. A few grandees, enriched by the patronage of the English court, might live magnificently

---

[1] See Paul Robert Lieder, 'Scott and Scandinavian Literature', in *Smith College Studies in Modern Languages* (Northampton, Mass.), Oct. 1920.

[2] I have dealt with this subject more fully in my essay 'The Scottish Enlightenment', in *Studies on Voltaire and the Eighteenth Century*, LVIII (Institut et Musée Voltaire, Geneva, 1967).

in their heavy, bizarre castles; but beneath them the gentry, generation after generation, lived on, the same ritual, predatory life, within their closed, traditional circle. Then, with the Union of 1707, came the change. First by trade with England, then by service in England, finally—and most of all in Scott's own time —by the vast patronage of India, the circle was broken. Like the Highlands after Culloden, but more gradually, the Borders became an 'open society'; and each area in turn found the poet who would romanticise its dissolving past.

It was in his childhood, at the farm of Sandy-knowe, near Smailholm tower, that Scott discovered his romantic attachment to the Border country. It was under an Oriental Plane-tree in a garden at Kelso that he read Percy's *Reliques*; and Percy and Goethe (says his son-in-law) were to be the inspiration of his whole life. It was under the influence of Percy that he would study the ballad literature of Northern Europe and set out, as a young lawyer, every year, on his 'raids' into Liddesdale, sometimes on horseback with his friend Shortreed, sometimes with his wife by phaëton—the first wheeled carriage ever to penetrate those rural valleys—in quest of those popular ballads which he would publish in 1802 as *Minstrelsy of the Scottish Border*—'the well', as Carlyle called it, 'from which flowed one of the broadest of rivers'. At the same time he was exploring the Highlands too, visiting old survivors of the Jacobite days before Culloden, studying the vanishing manners of Highland society, 'wasting his great talent', as his shocked old Presbyterian tutor complained, collecting 'ancient ballads and traditional stories about fairies, witches and ghosts',[1] and writing those original poems—*The Lay of the Last Minstrel, Marmion, The Lady of the Lake*—so unreadable today, which

---

[1] See the enjoyable account by Scott's old tutor, James Mitchell, in J. G. Lockhart, *Memoirs of Sir Walter Scott* (Library of English Classics, 1900), i, 87–94. Mitchell wasted *his* time, on the occasion of this meeting, trying to enlist Scott's patronage for 'the strict and evangelical party in the Church of Scotland'.

gave him his first fame. Before he had ever written a novel, Scott had eclipsed the two founding fathers of the romantic revival. He was at once the new Percy of his country, the new Ossian of his time.

Ballad literature, to the student of it, is inseparable from history: it is the direct expression of a historical form of society, which often has no other documents. In collecting the ballads of the past, Scott was re-creating and illustrating a vanished or vanishing society, and thereby, indirectly, becoming its historian. Nor was it only by such collection that he showed his historical interest. All his life he read history, re-created history, published the materials of history. Historians use his compilations still: his *Sadler State Papers*, his *Somers Tracts*, his reissues of arcane Stuart pamphlets. He founded the Bannatyne Club to publish Scottish Antiquities. At one time he planned 'a *corpus historiarum*, or full edition of the chronicles of England, an immense work', to rival the great collective work of the Benedictines of St Maur—a work for which Gibbon had once sighed and encouraged the Scottish historian Pinkerton to undertake.[1] But this vast enterprise remained a dream. It was not, perhaps, beyond Scott's powers—after all, Scott's edition of Dryden, in eighteen volumes, thrown off between poetry, essays and an active life in the law, was good enough to be reprinted *in toto* a century later—but ultimately Scott was not that kind of a historian. If he had been, he would by now be forgotten. For all his accuracy of detail, he was not a scholar: he was an imaginative historian who used his evidence not to document but to re-create the past. As Carlyle wrote in his Journal, on learning of Scott's death, 'he knew what *history* meant; this was his chief intellectual merit'[2]; and he found his

---

[1] Edward Gibbon, *Miscellaneous Works* (ed. 1837), pp. 836–42. George IV, who had a delicate taste in such matters, chose, as his gift to Scott, the 15 folio volumes of Montfaucon's *Antiquities* (Lockhart, op. cit., iv, 152).

[2] J. A. Froude, *Thomas Carlyle, A History of the First Forty Years of his Life* (new ed., 1890), ii, 321–22.

perfect medium when, after so many preliminary ventures, he produced, from 1814 onwards, his great historical novels, with their marvellous fusion of living persons and a reconstructed past: *Waverley, Guy Mannering, Old Mortality, Rob Roy, Heart of Midlothian....*

Above all, *Old Mortality*. What a wonderful work that is! What historian has ever so captured the character of pre-Union Scotland: of the fanatical Cameronians, of John Graham of Claverhouse, of the royalists and episcopalians and 'indulged ministers' of the Killing Times! Who that has once read it can ever forget the murder of archbishop Sharpe on Magus Moor, or Lady Margaret Bellenden and her Tower of Tillietudlem? It was a real work of scholarship as well as imagination, the first novel—as Lockhart remarks—in which Scott had to reach back beyond the date of human memory and reconstruct, from books alone, an unremembered past age.[1] And how well he reconstructed it! The professional historians did not like it. The Revd. Thomas McCrie, the learned biographer of John Knox and Andrew Melville, a strict dissenting Presbyterian, protested that Scott had libelled the Covenanters, and thundered away in the *Edinburgh Christian Instructor*. 'Spare not the vile Tory of an author!' the Christian editor adjured him; and he spared not. *Old Mortality*, wrote McCrie, was full of 'gross partiality and injustice... disfigured with profaneness... unjustifiable in any book, but altogether inexcusable in one that is intended for popular amusement'. Scott's greatest historical disciple, Macaulay, would afterwards present a very different picture of Claverhouse, as a man 'rapacious and profane, of violent temper and obdurate heart', rightly detested 'with a peculiar energy of hatred' by Scotsmen throughout the world. But time has vindicated the novelist, not the historians. The fanatical Covenanters are fanatics still, in spite of Dr McCrie and the long, dreary line of Kirk hagiographers. Macaulay's

---

[1] Lockhart, op. cit., iii, 84.

portrait of Claverhouse was exposed as a caricature by Paget and can never be restored.[1] Scott, whose imagination saw past the mere literary evidence, who envisaged the whole, compact, articulated society of Scotland in its years of crisis, and who looked daily on the portrait of Claverhouse,[2] saw, here at least, better than both.

In 1814, when Scott began to publish his novels, the public events of Europe had conspired to provide him with an audience. The nations were now in arms against Napoleon; Burke, not Voltaire was the political philosopher of the day; and historians were eager to describe not the mechanics of progress, which so easily led to revolution, but the robust vitalising spirit which fortified and preserved the legitimate organs, institutions, and traditions of the past. Moreover, in the countries of Europe—and particularly in Germany, which had never yielded to the 'philosophy' of the Encyclopaedists—the same romantic quest for reliques of ancient poetry had ended not only in the discovery of such poetry but in the creation, through it, of a new historical philosophy.

For in Germany, too, Percy as well as Ossian had his dis-

---

[1] McCrie's (anonymous) review of *Old Mortality*, 75,000 words long, was published in three successive numbers of the *Edinburgh Christian Instructor* (January–March 1817), and was afterwards reprinted, both as a separate book and in *The Miscellaneous Writings of Thomas McCrie* (1841). The editor of the *Christian Instructor* was the Revd. Andrew Thomson: his letter to McCrie is quoted in *Life of Thomas McCrie DD, by his son, the Revd. Thomas McCrie*, Edinburgh, 1840, p. 221. Scott replied (anonymously) in the *Quarterly Review*, April 1817. See also his (anonymous) review of Charles Kirkpatrick Sharpe's edition of James Kirkton's *Secret History of the Church of Scotland* in *Quarterly Review* 1818. Anyone who examines the matter will see that, although he made errors of detail, Scott used more and better sources than McCrie, and used them more critically and historically. McCrie (like Macaulay after him) ignored the best available source and relied exclusively on what Paget very properly described as 'the trash of Wodrow'. See John Paget, *The New Examen*, 1861: 'Viscount Dundee'.

[2] In the library of his house in Edinburgh Scott had only one picture: a portrait of Claverhouse, 'that beautiful and melancholy visage, worthy of the most pathetic dreams of romance'. Lockhart, op. cit., iii, 86.

ciples. The greatest of them, of course, was Herder: Herder the
philosophic founder of cultural history, the prophet of romantic nationalism, who saw the primitive poetry of every nation
as the direct expression of its distinguishing soul, the repository
of its autonomous history; and who, in his famous collection of
national songs, *Stimmen der Völker in Liedern*, published in
1778-79, included many translations both from Ossian and
from Percy's *Reliques*. But if Herder first proclaimed the new
doctrine in Germany, and made out of it a new philosophy of
history, it was not he who applied that philosophy. That was
done, first of all, not by philosophers or historians but by
classical philologists; and the new ballads which they discovered
or invented, came not from Germany but from ancient Greece
and Rome.

First there was Friedrich Voss whose translation of Homer
into German hexameters in the 1780s and 1790s so excited his
contemporaries. Then there was F. A. Wolf who, by his exact
philological scholarship on the Greek text, so dissolved the
unity of Homer that it has never been restored. To Wolf, the
creator of 'the Homeric question', the Iliad was not, as it had
been to all his predecessors, the majestic artefact of one great
blind poet: it was a later construction, pieced together, like
Macpherson's *Ossian*, out of numerous old Greek 'lays'; lays
exactly comparable with the popular ballads now published by
Percy and Herder. Wolf's exciting doctrine was published in
1795. A few years later its historical implications were drawn
out and applied by the most revolutionary historian of the
nineteenth century. This innovator was the lifelong friend of
Voss, the devout disciple of Wolf: the North German scholar-
banker, Barthold Georg Niebuhr.

Like Scott, Niebuhr was a Borderer, strongly attached to his
childhood home. He was brought up in Dithmarschen, on the
Danish border, among the historic recollections of an ancient
peasant republic whose stubborn conservative resistance against

the Dukes of Holstein was commemorated in popular ballads. All his life Niebuhr remembered Dithmarschen and its solid rural independent conservatism. All his life he was interested in ancient popular poetry. He translated a modern Greek folk-song and proposed to translate the newly published Serbian ballads.[1] He regarded the recently discovered *Nibelungenlied*[2] as the greatest of poems. In Latin literature he despised Vergil as a feeble, artificial court poet. Even Ennius, the rude father of Latin Poetry, seemed to him too aristocratic, too literary; for was there not evidence that, before Ennius, the primitive Roman republic, like the autonomous republic of Dithmarschen or the oppressed peoples of the Balkans, had possessed still ruder and therefore better ballads which Ennius, with his Greek metres, had driven out of memory? Then, in a moment of inspiration, 'a sudden flash of light', sparked off by Wolf's treatment of Homer,[3] Niebuhr saw a new solution to an old problem.

That problem concerned the sources of early Roman history. The only continuous native literary evidence for that history was the work of Livy. But what evidence, men asked, had Livy himself used? The official records of Rome had been destroyed in 389 B.C., when the city was taken by the Gauls. How then could Livy narrate, in such details, events two and three centuries even before that date? Already in the late seventeenth century the Dutch scholar Perizonius had raised this question and had suggested an answer: Livy had drawn his matter from

[1] The Greek ballads were collected and published by Claude Charles Fauriel (*Chants Populaires de la Grèce Moderne*, Paris, 1824). A German translation by Wilhelm Müller appeared at Leipzig in 1825. For the Serbian ballads see below, p. 15.

[2] The ms. of the *Nibelungenlied* had been discovered in 1755, in the library of Hohenems, in the Upper Rhineland, by J. H. Obereit. It was published in 1756–57 by J. J. Bodmer.

[3] 'Das Wichtigste ist das Ergebnis plötzlicher Lichtblike und Divinationen', Niebuhr wrote in a letter of 20 December 1829 (*Lebensnachrichten über B. G. Niebuhr . . .*, Hamburg, 1838–39), iii, 248 ff.

popular 'lays' transmitted orally from generation to generation.[1] But Perizonius had no direct knowledge of such 'lays'.
He wrote before Ossian was known or Percy had published, or
the *Nibelungenlied* had been recovered. His suggestion was
therefore a hypothesis only. But now, exclaimed Niebuhr, the
hypothesis had been put 'on firm ground' by the happy dis-
coveries of the philologists. 'For us the heroic lays of Spain,
Scotland, and Scandinavia have long been a common stock;
the song of the Nibelungs has already returned and taken its
place in literature; and now that we listen to the Serbian lays
and to those of Greece, the swan-like strains of a slaughtered
nation; now that everyone knows how poetry lives in every
people' (the words might be taken straight from Herder), until
art stifles it, 'the empty objections' made to Perizonius' theory
'no longer need any answer': the case is self-evident.[2] Having
reached this conclusion, Niebuhr looked again at Livy, and
under that smooth, milky text his eye divined, and his critical
scholarship disengaged, the very form and structure, the titles,
even the words, of a whole cycle of lays; and from those lays,
in turn, he deduced the character of the society which created
them: the popular, conservative republic of Rome.

Niebuhr's achievement—his imaginative use of exact critical
methods to revise the history of the past—inspired all the historians of the nineteenth century, even those who rebelled at
the dogmatism of his conclusions. He was the father of con-
structive historical *Quellenkritik*. His method, one English
historian wrote, was like 'Ithuriel's spear' at whose touch false-
hood was transformed to truth.[3] But he also did, more scienti-
fically, in his historical writing, what Scott had done in his

---

[1] Jacobus Perizonius, *Animadversiones Historicae* (Amsterdam, 1685),
caput VI.

[2] Niebuhr, *The History of Rome*, transl. by J. C. Hare and Connop Thirlwall (Cambridge, 1828), i, 212–18.

[3] Charles Beard, *The Reformation of the 16th Century* (1883, reprint Ann
Arbor, 1962), p. 346.

novels. Both used a new insight to reconstruct, out of hitherto neglected material, the vanished context of formal history. Implicit in the work of both was a new historical philosophy. Unlike the classical 'philosophic historians', they saw the successive ages of the past not as mere stages in the history of progress, whose value lay in their relevance to the present, but as self-sufficient totalities of human life, valid within their own terms, demanding from the historian neither praise nor blame but sympathetic, imaginative re-creation. Such re-creation required effort. The historian must breathe the atmosphere of the past, think in its mental categories. He may not, like the 'philosophical historians' of the Enlightenment, insulate himself in his library in London or Paris, Edinburgh or Lausanne. Voltaire, for all his universal claims, had never stepped down from his eighteenth-century elevation. Even Gibbon, for all his submerged romanticism, had never visited any part of that Byzantine Empire whose millennial history he had written. No nineteenth-century historian would dare to show such sublime insouciance. The reality of the past, the historical value of its spontaneous, popular expression, its local and temporal colour, would be respected alike, though with different emphasis, by radical and conservative, whig and tory: Michelet and Carlyle, Macaulay and Ranke.[1]

Consider the greatest of conservative historians, perhaps the greatest of all historians in the nineteenth century, Leopold von Ranke. At first it might seem difficult to discover romanticism in this austere, dispassionate scholar. Technically, indeed, Ranke was a disciple of Niebuhr. Niebuhr's book, he wrote, was the first German historical work to excite him by

---

[1] Fritz Renker, *Niebuhr und die Romantik* (Leipzig, 1935) seeks to dissociate Niebuhr from the Romantic Movement by emphasising his classical interests and his sound Protestant views, as opposed to what Niebuhr himself called 'das Katholicisieren und die Überschwenglichkeit der romantischen Schule'. By that definition Scott was not a romantic either.

opening new historical horizons, and time only increased his respect for that 'magnanimous spirit', that 'great Master of Antiquity'. At the age of ninety Ranke would still look back on Wolf and Niebuhr as 'our classics, who illuminated my youthful steps'.[1] In his own rigorous *Quellenkritik* Ranke proves the truth of this claim. But it was not only a critical spirit that Ranke shared with Niebuhr. He too was a conservative, revolting, in historical scholarship as in politics, against the tyranny of French ideas; and he too looked to native popular literature as the authentic, direct expression of autonomous societies or past ages.

At first Ranke, like so many lesser historians,[2] was seduced by that universal enchanter, Sir Walter Scott. In his autobiography he tells us how, in those years, Scott's novels were being read all over Europe, and were inspiring sympathy with past times. He too read and was excited by them. Admittedly, the excitement did not last. *Quentin Durward* broke the charm. Scott's Louis XI and Charles the Bold, Ranke discovered, did not tally with those of Commines and other contemporary writers, and he decided to pursue truth, not romance. So 'I turned altogether away and resolved, in my work, to avoid all imagination, all poetry, and keep firmly to the facts'.[3] In his first published work, at the age of twenty-nine, he declared this resolution. His aim, he then wrote, was not to judge the past, but simply to show it 'wie es eigentlich gewesen'.[4] Nevertheless, this rejection of romance was not absolute. A few years later

---

[1] Ranke, *Sämmtliche Werke*, vols. 53–54, *Zur Eigenen Lebensgeschichte* (Leipzig, 1900), p. 31; *Briefwerk* (Hamburg, 1949), pp. 69–70; *Neue Briefe* (Hamburg, 1949), pp. 264, 484, 737.

[2] e.g. Augustin Thierry, whose *Histoire de la Conquête de l'Angleterre par les Normands* (1825), as Eduard Fueter says (*Geschichte der neueren Historiographie*, Berlin, 1925, p. 445), could hardly have been written without Scott's *Ivanhoe* (1820).

[3] Ranke, *Zur Eigenen Lebensgeschichte*, p. 61.

[4] Ranke, *Sämmtliche Werke*, vols. 33–44, *Geschichten der romanischen und germanischen Völker*, Preface.

it was to return, in a new form: direct, as Scott himself had received it, from a popular source.

In 1827, at the age of thirty-two, Ranke went to Vienna and there gained access to the Venetian *Relazioni* preserved in the *Hofbibliothek*. The Keeper of the Library, at that time, was Jernej (Bartholomäus) Kopitar, a Slovene who was interested in the popular literature of the South Slavs. Fifteen years earlier, Kopitar had been Metternich's censor of Slavonic languages and in that capacity had opened and read letters written in Slavonic. By this unusual method of patronage he had discovered, in Vienna, a Serbian *émigré* who was seeking to revive the half-forgotten Serbo-croat language. Kopitar had sought out and encouraged his victim, who, thanks to that encouragement, became the greatest figure in the literary history of Yugoslavia, the re-creator of its language, the collector and publisher of its historic ballads, Vuk Stefanović Karadžić. Through Kopitar, Ranke met Vuk himself, and Vuk showed him all his documents concerning the recent Serbian revolt, which he had witnessed. Ranke was fascinated by them. The historian who had turned away from the romantic novelist, from the editor of *The Minstrelsy of the Scottish Border*, found himself entranced by 'the most learned of all Serbs', the editor of the *Pesnarica*.

When Ranke discovered Vuk, he forgot or postponed his work on the Venetian *Relazioni*. He decided, with Vuk's aid, to write a history of the Serbian revolt. Every day the two men sat together at a table going through Vuk's papers, and Vuk told Ranke about the Serbian ballads which he had collected and which another common friend in Vienna, Wenzeslaw Hanka, had translated into German. The result of their collaboration was Ranke's *History of the Revolution in Serbia*, which appeared in 1828 and contained a chapter on Serbian popular culture and Serbian ballads. It was read by Niebuhr who declared that that little book was 'the best that we have in our literature' (*das vortrefflichste was wir in unsrer Literatur besitzen*). When this verdict was reported to Ranke he was delighted: it was, he wrote, 'an antidote to all calumny'.[1]

Ranke never forgot Vuk, or his debt to him—though his biographers and critics do not think it worth mentioning. To him Serbian history and Serbian ballads were as significant as the history and ballads of Dithmarschen had been to Niebuhr. Fifty years later he would recall how 'my unforgettable friend Vuk' would come every day, stumping with his wooden leg up the stairway in Vienna, to bring to the historian a new supply of Serbian records, Serbian ballads, Serbian reminiscences.[2]

So much for Ranke. Now let us turn from the greatest of conservative historians to the greatest of whigs. No two contemporary historians could be more opposite from each other than Ranke and Macaulay. They had a common tradition, of course. Both were heirs of the Enlightenment. But they inherited different parts of that tradition. Ranke inherited its universal spirit, from which however he abstracted its driving motor of progress, believing (like Herder) in the autonomy of the past and the equal rights of all cultures: every age, as he put it, was 'immediate to God'. Macaulay believed intensely in that motor and drove it fast, respecting no such rights. History, to him, was 'emphatically the history of Progress', and the past only mattered, in the last analysis, in so far as it illustrated that process. As Ranke complained, Macaulay constantly summoned the past before the bar of the present to be judged and condemned. And yet Macaulay, like Ranke, was deeply influenced by the new spirit—though, once again, with a difference. While the conservative, academic Ranke turned away from the warm but dangerous imagination of Scott to the exact

---

[1] Ranke, *Zur Eigenen Lebensgeschichte,* p. 64; *Briefwerk,* pp. 166, 174, 204, 269; *Neue Briefe,* 153. For Kopitar and Vuk see D. Subotić, *Yugoslav Popular Ballads* (Cambridge, 1932), p. 9.

[2] Ranke, *Zur Eigenen Lebensgeschichte,* p. 621.

criticism of Niebuhr, the whig politician Macaulay, while moving within the same field, moved in the opposite direction. He was first captivated, then disillusioned by Niebuhr; but for all his whiggism, and his almost pathological hatred of the Stuarts, he never ceased to be a disciple of the romantic Jacobite tory, whose politics, ideas, and way of life he uniformly deplored, Sir Walter Scott.[1]

Macaulay, like Ranke, was a young man when Scott's novels were conquering the world and, like Ranke, he was captivated by them. He also saw that they provided new opportunities to the writer of history, and in 1828 he said so. In that year he published, in the *Edinburgh Review*, an essay on 'History'. It is not a profound essay, and he did not afterwards include it in his collected essays[2]; but it contains, for our purpose, an interesting passage. It is the passage in which he discusses the qualities of the ideal historian.

It is interesting to compare Macaulay's profession of historical faith, at the age of twenty-eight, with that which Ranke had published four years earlier, at the age of twenty-nine. There is nothing here of austere objectivity, of the natural rights of the past. And yet the past was not to be entirely subordinated to the present. It might be indulged in inessentials. Like an 'autonomous' republic under the firm rule of Muscovite orthodoxy, it might at least keep its quaint local costumes, its country dances, its dialect, its cheeses. The ideal historian, says Macaulay, should not confine himself to formal narrative, but should enliven his account of public events by interspersing in

---

[1] For Macaulay's strong disapproval of Scott's way of life see Sir G. O. Trevelyan, *Life and Letters of Lord Macaulay* (World's Classics), i, 438. The complacent panegyrist of the bourgeois virtues and suburban villas of provincial England naturally deplored the genial feudal extravagance of the new laird of Abbotsford. Scott (in Macaulay's eyes) should have settled down in Edinburgh and been a good, steady, solvent whig.

[2] It is published in the Albany Edition of *The Works of Lord Macaulay* (1900), vol. vii.

it 'the details which are the charm of historical romances'. Then, after telling the story of the apprentice of Lincoln who made, for the cathedral, out of fragments rejected by his master, a stained-glass window so fine that 'the vanquished artist killed himself from mortification', he goes on: 'Sir Walter Scott, in the same manner, has used those fragments of truth which historians have scornfully thrown behind them, in a manner which may well excite their envy. He has constructed out of their gleanings works which, even considered as histories, are scarcely less valuable than theirs. But a truly great historian would reclaim those materials which the novelist has appropriated': he would blend Clarendon with *Old Mortality*, Hume with *The Fortunes of Nigel*.

About the same time, Macaulay told his sister about his own historical method. 'My accuracy as to facts', he said, 'I owe to a cause which many men would not confess. It is due to my love of castle-building. The past is in my mind soon constructed into a romance.' Then he went on to describe how, on his solitary London walks, he constantly envisaged the scenes of the past: how every detail was visually imagined, every building exactly reconstructed, every place accurately peopled. 'I seem to know every inch of Whitehall. I go in at Hans Holbein's gate, and come out through the matted gallery. The conversations which I compose between great people of the time are long and sufficiently animated: in the style, if not with the merits, of Sir Walter Scott's.'[1] This same quality, this visual identification and localisation of past history, is shown in a comment which Macaulay made a few years later about Vergil: 'I like him best on Italian ground. I like his localities; his national enthusiasm; his frequent allusions to his country, its history, its antiquities, and its greatness. In this respect he often reminded me of Sir Walter Scott.'[2]

In the same years in which Macaulay was thus borrowing

[1] Trevelyan, op. cit., i, 170.   [2] Ibid., i, 343.

the historical method of Scott, he found his way, through the translation of Hare and Thirlwall, to the revolutionary work of Niebuhr. Though not, like some of his friends, 'Niebuhr-mad', Macaulay recognised at once that 'the appearance of the book is really an era in the intellectual history of Europe'.[1] He was particularly delighted with Niebuhr's idea of a cycle of Roman lays—lays which, even more than his favourite passages of Vergil, would obviously cling to Italian ground. But as yet Macaulay had not visited Italy. When he did go to Italy, in 1839, on his return from India, he was disillusioned with Niebuhr—the bold whig could not endure that timid conservatism, the dogmatist that rival dogmatism[2]—but the lays were still vivid in his mind, and when he saw the castellated hills and historic lakes of Tuscany, as romantic to a classical scholar as the river Tweed and Cheviot hills to a Borderer, a new project formed in his mind. Niebuhr and Scott, the Roman lays and the Border ballads, were suddenly fused together. Niebuhr, with his usual confidence, had already declared the exact subject of those lays: 'the history of Romulus, the story of Horatius, the destruction of Alba, above all "the lay of Tarquinius", culminating in the truly Homeric battle of Lake Regillus'. This last, wrote Niebuhr confidently, was the greatest of all, and 'should anyone ever have the boldness to think of restoring it in poetical form', he should cast it in the form of its only worthy rival, the *Nibelungenlied*.[3] Macaulay had that boldness. He wrote his *Lays of Ancient Rome*. They were the very lays which Niebuhr had named. In his preface he paid his tribute to Niebuhr. But the style of his poems was not that of the *Nibelungenlied*: it was that of the poems of Sir Walter Scott.

Thereafter Macaulay settled down to his great *History*, and sought to realise the ideal which he had set out in 1828. That whole work is indeed deeply influenced by Scott—not of course

[1] Ibid., i, 181.   [2] Ibid., i, 404–5.
[3] Niebuhr, *Roman History*, i, 220.

in its intellectual direction, but in its method and incidental illustration: its skilful use of local colour, trivial anecdote, and popular literature. No modern critic, that I know of, has mentioned this intimate dependence of Macaulay on Scott; but once mentioned, it is obvious, and contemporaries, who knew their Scott, quickly recognised it. In Ireland, Scott's old friend Maria Edgworth was still living at Edgworthstown, in county Longford. She it was who, by her Irish stories, had first inspired Scott to write his Waverley novels. Now, at the age of eighty-two, she read a presentation copy of Macaulay's first volume. Only one complaint qualified her delight: 'there is no mention of Sir Walter Scott throughout the whole work', even in places where it seemed impossible to avoid paying so obvious a tribute.[1] In England, a more critical commentator was another old friend of Scott, J. W. Croker. 'We suspect', he wrote, 'that we can trace Mr. Macaulay's design to its true source—the example and success of the author of Waverley. The historical novel, if not invented, at least first developed and illustrated by the happy genius of Scott', had taken 'a sudden and extensive hold of the public taste.' The press, since his time, had 'groaned with his imitators'. 'We have had served up in this form the Norman conquest and the Wars of the Roses, the Gunpowder Plot and the Fire of London, Darnley and Richelieu.' Harrison Ainsworth had just published 'a professed romance' on Macaulay's historical villain James II. 'Nay, on a novelist of this popular order has been conferred the office of *historiographer* to the Queen.'[2]

What was the quality, in Macaulay's writing, that proved, to these critics, the influence of Scott? First of all, there was Scott's great innovation, local colour. I have mentioned Macaulay's strong sense of 'locality', the association of events

---

[1] Quoted in Trevelyan, ii, 172.

[2] J. W. Croker in *Quarterly Review*, lxxxiv (March, 1849), 551. The historiographer royal was G. P. R. James, an imitator of Scott. He was the author of *Richelieu, Darnley*, and over sixty other historical novels.

with places: a sense which he appreciated in Vergil and explicitly associated with Scott. In all his own writing he showed this sense—in his Indian essays as in his Italian 'lays'—and he gratified it fully in his *History*. When writing his *History*, Macaulay did not sit continuously in his library. He travelled abroad. He visited not only the archives but the scenes: the marshlands of Sedgemoor, the town of Torbay, the battlefields of Flanders, Scotland, Ireland. He saw with his own eyes Londonderry and the Boyne, Glencoe and Killiecrankie, and peopled them, as he had long ago peopled Whitehall and Hampton Court, with their historic actors. In so doing, he gave life to the past even if—since Macaulay's vices are never very far from his virtues—he could not resist the temptation to reiterate, every time, the vast improvement which 'whig' progress had brought to the marshes and towns of the West Country, the bogs of Ireland, and the waste Highlands of Scotland.

Moreover, Macaulay drew this life from the same sources as Scott: from the neglected informal, popular literature of the time. He had no patience with those who talked of 'the dignity of history'.[1] Like Scott, he was a great browser in bookshops, a voracious reader in the byways of literature. He read comedies and farces, lampoons and satires, broadsheets and ballads. He went through the Pepysian ballads in Magdalene College, Cambridge; he dug out the un-indexed Roxburghe Ballads in the British Museum; he used the success of *Lilliburlero* to illustrate the unpopularity of Tyrconnel in Protestant Ireland, and a bogus ballad planted upon him "in a most obliging manner' by a clergyman at Morwenstow to illustrate the popularity of bishop Trelawney in Cornwall.[2] In this way he realised his old ambition to reclaim for history 'those materials which the novelist has appropriated'.

---

[1] Trevelyan, op. cit., ii, 55–56.
[2] On the obliging Rev. R. S. Hawker of Morenstow, see the article in *D.N.B.*

A dangerous ambition! we may exclaim, as we look back at a century and more of romantic historiography: as we read the purpler passages of Carlyle, Froude and Freeman, Motley, Prescott, and Parkman; as we think of the long decline of what the French called *histoire Walter Scottée* into the 'tushery' of Victorian novelists and those local pageants which were organised by Louis-Napoleon Parker and ridiculed, but not killed, by J. H. Round. How much better, we may think, is that other, opposite product of the Romantic movement in history, the austere, self-denying spirit of Ranke, who sought to sever the past from the present, to avoid not merely modern prejudice but even imagination and poetry, and to pursue only an unattainable objectivity! How much better still, we may conclude, are the pre-romantic historians, the enlightened, 'philosophical' historians of the eighteenth century, who, since they did not deaden the past by severing it from the present, had no need either to embalm it in the cold, stately mausoleum of German conservatism, or to jerk it into spurious life by imposing on it their synthetic colours and ventriloqual sounds! Both Ranke and Macaulay, by their romantic borrowings—the one by his almost sterilised conservatism, the other by his distorting vitality—may be said, like the Romantic movement in general, to have put the clock of European thought not forward but back. Has not Ranke been accused of having, by his passive, academic 'objectivity', contributed indirectly to the rise of that German Nazism to which Carlyle, by his romantic hero-worship, directly pointed the way? Did not Macaulay, by his compelling narrative, by his decorative romantic detail superimposed on a purely political study, distract historians from that profounder analysis which the disciples of Montesquieu had made possible but which was only resumed, a century later, by the disciples of Marx?

So we may say; but to what purpose? Genius is not responsible for the botcheries of its imitators, nor should we judge new ideas by their distorted consequences. No great movement is pure; advance in any one field is often purchased by retreat in another; and every new gospel introduces a train of superstitions, sometimes grosser than those which it has displaced. Ideas are to be valued not by their incidental corruptions, but by their permanence, their power to survive those corruptions. If we are to judge the contribution of romanticism to historical study, we should try to isolate what was permanent in it, and view it at its best.

The historiography of the Enlightenment, at its best, had been animated by 'philosophy'. The eighteenth-century historians looked back and saw a new meaning in the past. They saw history as a process, and a process, moreover, of improvement, of 'progress'. Thereby they gave to its study a new value, not merely moral and political, but intellectual and social. But if they thus penetrated to the inner meaning of history, they did so, too often, by overlooking its human content. The men of the past entered their story only indirectly, as the agents or victims of 'progress': they seldom appeared directly, in their own right, in their own social context, as the legitimate owners of their own autonomous centuries. The romantic writers changed all that. Seeing the doctrine of progress converted from a gospel of humanity into a slogan of conquest, they cast it aside and tried to look on the past direct. Whether, like Ranke, they altogether rejected the concept of progress as merely distorting their new vision, or, like Macaulay, adjusted their new vision in order to embellish that concept, they resolved, at all costs, to make the past live. As Carlyle wrote of Sir Walter Scott who is the real hero of this lecture (but I did not dare put him in the title lest his very name should frighten away the audience), he first showed 'the old life of men resuscitated for us. . . . Not as dead tradition but as palpable presence, the past stood before us'. Scott's historical novels, said Carlyle, 'have taught all men this truth, which looks like a truism, and yet was as good as unknown to writers of history and others, till so taught: that the bygone ages of the world were actually filled by living men, not by protocols, state-papers, controversies, and abstractions of men'.[1] That surely is a permanent truth which, however it may be corrupted, historians can never afford to forget.

[1] Carlyle, *Critical and Miscellaneous Essays*, 'Sir Walter Scott'.